The Cricket

This book has been reviewed
for accuracy by
Walter L. Gojmerac
Professor of Entomology
University of Wisconsin—Madison.

Library of Congress Cataloging in Publication Data

Hasegawa, Yō.
The cricket.

(Nature close-ups)
Translation of: Kōrogi / text by Yō Hasegawa,
photographs by Hidekazu Kubo.
Summary: Text and photographs describe the life
cycle, behavior, and natural habitat of crickets.
1. Crickets—Juvenile literature. [1. Crickets]
I. Kubo, Hidekazu, ill. II. Title. III. Series.
QL508.G8H37 1986 595.7′26 85-28201

ISBN 0-8172-2532-3 (lib. bdg.)
ISBN 0-8172-2557-9 (softcover)

This edition first published in 1986 by Raintree Publishers Inc.

1 2 3 4 5 6 7 8 9 0 90 89 88 87 86

◀ **A cricket nymph peeking above the ground.**

▶ **Two newly emerged cricket nymphs.**

These nymphs are still fragile, but they will grow stronger and darker each day. Because the nymph looks just like the adult at this stage of its development, the cricket is said to go through an incomplete metamorphosis. Insects that have an additional pupal stage are said to undergo a complete metamorphosis.

In the springtime, baby crickets, called nymphs, emerge from eggs which have been underground all winter. The nymphs are covered with a thin film that protects their soft, fragile bodies as they move about in the earth. After they have burrowed their way to the earth's surface, the nymphs discard the film and stretch their legs and antennae. The nymphs have no wings and are light in color. Otherwise they look like adult crickets.

● **Cricket eggs in spring.**

When eggs are laid in fall, they are pale yellow and less than one-tenth of an inch long. The female cricket deposits her eggs about one-half inch deep in the earth. By the time they are ready to hatch in the spring, the bodies of the young nymphs can be seen inside the eggs.

◀ **A nymph in hiding.**

Often, many cricket nymphs live together in the same hiding place. This nymph is peeking out from a hole in a bank of earth.

▶ **A nymph in a tree stump.**

Because the young cricket spends most of the day hiding, its eyes are not well developed. It uses its antennae to touch objects and to detect odors. The feelers are slender and flexible and easily fit into narrow spaces where the cricket creeps.

It takes a month, sometimes longer, for a nymph to grow to adulthood. During that time, the fragile young cricket's life is always in danger. A variety of ground bugs and beetles eat both unhatched cricket eggs and young nymphs. In order to escape their enemies, cricket nymphs spend a lot of their time hiding—under dried grasses or beneath rocks or in holes in the ground.

● **As it matures, the nymph grows darker.**

As the fragile, light-colored nymph (photo 1) eats and grows, it changes in color. In this species, the nymph's body turns black and has a white stripe across its back (photo 2).

◀ **Cricket nymphs eating an eggplant.**

These nymphs have antennae that are much longer than their bodies. The two cerci which extend from the back of the cricket help it to sense movement and possible approaching danger.

▶ **Crickets feeding on a dead earthworm.**

Crickets have large, pincer-like jaws for chewing up food.

The amount of time it takes for a nymph to mature depends on the weather conditions, the species of cricket, and what kind of food it eats. Adults of the same species may vary in size, depending on the diet of the developing nymph.

Crickets eat just about anything they can find—bits of fruits and vegetables, small insects, grain, scraps of wool and other cloth. The cricket nymph comes out from hiding at night to search for food. It uses antennae to detect food. It may find an eggplant in a garden or a dead earthworm in a field.

Crickets have strong, pincer-like jaws for chewing. They use small, movable feelers, called palpi, to find food nearby and to tell whether the food is good to eat.

● **A nymph molting (photos 1-4).**

When the nymph has outgrown its old exoskeleton, it attaches itself to a leaf or twig and begins to molt. When it first emerges from the old skin, the nymph's new skin is light in color. Soon it will darken and harden.

As the nymph eats and becomes larger, it outgrows its hard, outer skin, called an exoskeleton. So, it must molt, or shed, its skin. A nymph molts several times as it grows. The nymph attaches itself to a leaf or twig or blade of grass and remains still. The old skin splits down the back and the nymph crawls out, as light in color as when it first emerged from the egg. Because it cannot move during the molting process, this is a dangerous time for the nymph. Enemies may attack it. One cricket nymph may even eat another as it is molting.

◀ **A nymph eating its old skin.**

Once it has molted, the nymph turns around and eats the discarded skin. It contains nutrients, which make it a healthy meal.

▶ **A nymph that has just molted.**

A cricket may molt seven or more times, depending on the species, before it becomes an adult.

2

3

4

◀ **Ground beetles attacking a nymph.**

Crickets are always in danger, even in their hiding places. Ground beetles and bugs live in the same places crickets do. They are the cricket's natural enemies, or predators.

Although adult crickets vary in size and color, they all have the same basic body structure. Three pairs of jointed legs and two pairs of wings are attached to the middle part of the body, the thorax. The hind legs are the largest and strongest and enable the cricket to jump great distances. A tiny, one-inch cricket can travel as far as two feet in one leap. Two sense organs, called cerci, extend from the back part of the cricket's body, the abdomen.

● **A male (left) and a female nymph (right).**

It is difficult to tell a male nymph from a female when they have first emerged from the eggs. But after a few moltings, the female begins to grow an ovipositor, a long tube for laying eggs. The ovipositor extends from the tip of the abdomen.

▼ A cricket nymph chewing on a stalk.

Sharp spines pointed backward on the cricket's legs help it to scramble among blades of grass and give it a firmer grip on leaves, stems, and stalks.

● **A cricket emerging as an adult (photos 1-5).**

In its final molt, as in previous ones, the cricket's skin is light in color when it first emerges from the old exoskeleton. The arrow in photo 3 shows a spiracle, an opening in the abdomen through which the cricket breathes.

When the nymph is fully grown, it prepares to go through its final molting. As it did in previous moltings, it fixes itself to a stalk or twig. The old exoskeleton splits down the back and the cricket slowly comes out. First the head appears, then the thorax. The tiny wing pads, which had formed in earlier stages of the nymph's development, are now fully developed as two pairs of wings. Then come the legs, and finally, the long, segmented abdomen. When the old exoskeleton has been completely shed, the cricket has entered the last stage in its life cycle. It is now a winged adult.

As it has done in previous moltings, the adult cricket eats the old skin. Then the cricket unfolds its crumpled wings. As they stretch out, they harden and dry.

4

5

◀ **An adult cricket eating a tomato.**

Generally, crickets come out of hiding at night, in search of food. This cricket is eating a juicy ripe tomato.

▶ **Crickets peeping out from a can.**

Before long, the adult cricket's skin will darken and harden. Its tough, shell-like exoskeleton and its ability to jump quickly away from enemies are its only defenses. Birds, rodents, toads, frogs, and snakes are all predators of the cricket. So the adult spends a great deal of time in hiding. Often, nymphs and adults are seen together in the same hiding places.

Like the nymph, the adult cricket eats just about anything it can find. But while the young cricket eats in order to grow larger, the adult cricket eats so it will have energy to mate and reproduce.

▶ **Crickets in hiding.**

When a cricket detects vibrations with its ear tympanums, or senses danger with its cerci, it goes into hiding—not always successfully.

▲ Crickets call to one another across this field in autumn at sunset.

In late summer or early fall, the evening air is filled with the sound of crickets chirping. The music of these winged singers carries a variety of messages long distance to fellow crickets. Only male crickets chirp. They have different songs for different occasions.

● **Crickets chirping.**

Most winged insects use their wings for flying, but crickets use them to make sounds. They do so by rubbing their wings together. Only male crickets chirp.

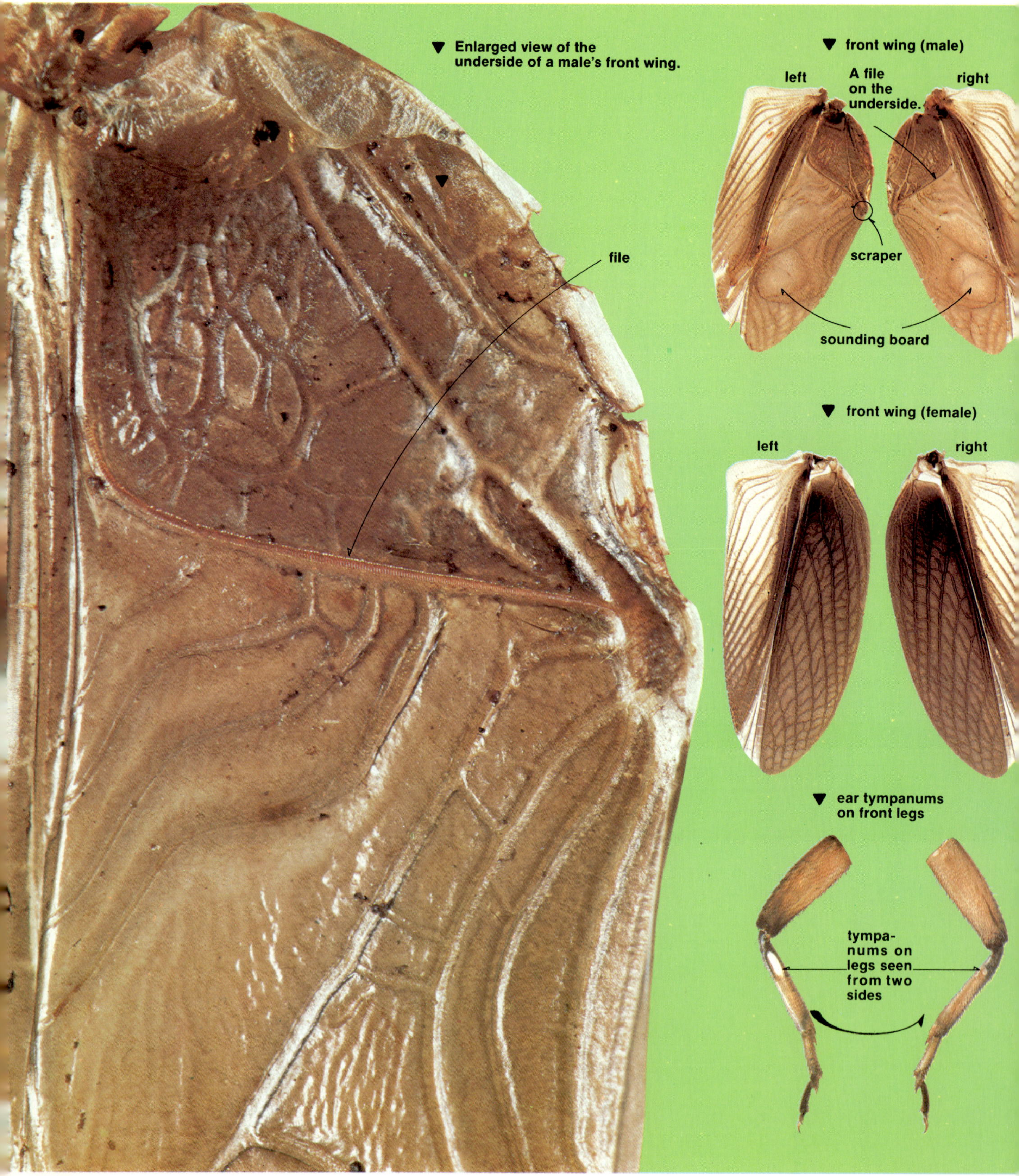
▼ Enlarged view of the underside of a male's front wing.
file
▼ front wing (male)
left
right
A file on the underside.
scraper
sounding board
▼ front wing (female)
left
right
▼ ear tympanums on front legs
tympanums on legs seen from two sides

The male cricket's wings are well suited for making sounds. On the underside of one front wing, there is a file, a thick vein with many tiny ridges. On the upper side of the opposite wing there is a scraper, a hardened vein. When the file is drawn across the scraper, a chirping sound is produced. A sounding board, a smooth area near the middle of each wing, vibrates to increase the sound.

By rubbing harder or softer, or by changing the angle of the wings, the males can change the meaning of their songs. Scientists tell us that there are three kinds of cricket chirps. The *regular* chirp is used to claim territory and to call to females. A *courtship* chirp is used to further attract the female crickets. And a *fighting* chirp is used by males to challenge one another.

▶ **Male crickets fighting** (photos 1-2).

When two males confront one another, they make strong chirping sounds. One male tries to drive off the other by pushing at it with its head. When one male has fought off the other, both crickets stop chirping.

The male cricket's courting song is quite different from the harsh chirping sounds he uses to fight off rivals. The sweet and gentle courting song is the one that is most often heard on warm autumn nights. The female cricket "hears" the song as the tympanums on her front legs detect its vibrations. By following the sound of his call, she knows exactly where to find the male cricket, even though he may be hidden in tall grass.

A cricket of another species cannot recognize this mating song and will not respond to it. This ensures that only crickets of the same species will mate with one another.

● **Crickets courting (photos 1-3).**

After being courted by his song, the female cricket sometimes leads the male in a playful chase before the two mate.

▼ Two crickets greeting one another (photo 4).

As the male and female come closer together, they examine one another's face and antennae. This may be another way crickets have of making sure they belong to the same species.

4

◀ **A male (bottom) and female (top) mating.**

▶ **A female cricket with bags of sperm.**

The cricket at the top has received white bags of sperm from a male. By autumn, female crickets are so heavy with eggs they are almost dragging their abdomens on the ground.

When crickets mate, the male creeps backward beneath the female. He attaches small white bags of sperm to her underside. Later, the sperm find their way inside the female's abdomen, where they are stored. Eventually, the sperm join with the eggs, which become fertilized.

The male and female stay together for hours after mating. He may chirp a special song to her during this time. The female will not respond to the courting song of another male until all her eggs have been deposited in the ground.

◀ **A female cricket with many eggs.**

Part of this cricket's abdomen has been removed to show how many eggs she has stored inside. If all the eggs laid by crickets became adults, there soon would be too many crickets in the world. But most of the eggs will be eaten by predators or will not last through the cold winter.

◀ **A female laying her eggs.**

A cricket may lay several hundred eggs in all. Most of the eggs or the young nymphs will be eaten by enemies or will die from disease or the harsh winter. Only a few will live to become adults.

◀ **A cricket egg laid in the ground.**

▶ **A dead cricket in autumn.**

Generally, after the female cricket has finished laying her eggs, she dies. In fact, almost all crickets die when freezing temperatures set in. But in spring, a new generation of crickets will emerge from the eggs.

After the female cricket has mated, she searches for a place to lay her eggs. She uses the needle-like ovipositor at the tip of her abdomen to drill holes into the earth. In each hole, about a half-inch deep, she deposits a tiny, yellow, banana-shaped egg. Then she carefully covers the holes.

In the ground, the eggs are protected from the cold winter weather. Although the eggs will lie still until spring, tiny cricket nymphs are already beginning to form inside. If they survive their predators and the cold, a new generation of crickets will emerge in springtime.

The Orthopteran Order

Scientists put crickets, locusts, and grasshoppers in the same category, or order, because they resemble each other in many ways. They all live in similar places, under dried grasses and beneath stones. Their flat bodies fit into narrow spaces and their body colors blend with their environment. Members of the Orthopteran order have biting mouth parts and usually two pairs of wings. They also have slender, flexible antennae and well-developed legs for jumping. These insects go through an incomplete metamorphosis.

Resemblances among species.

Even though these are the heads of three different species of crickets, they all look similar. Only the size and colors vary. Notice the large compound eyes, the slender antennae, and the small feelers, called palpi, which are used like hands in holding food as the cricket eats.

Where do crickets lay eggs?

Most crickets lay their eggs in the ground, but the females of the species below deposit their eggs on the grass or in trees.

1

2

3

Not all crickets have common names. The crickets in these photos are identified by their scientific names:

(**1**) *Scapsipedus aspersus*
(**2**) *Loxoblemmus arietulus*
(**3**) *Loxoblemmus doenitzi*
(**4**) *Homoegryllus japonicus*
(**5**) *Pteronemobius fascipes*
(**6**) *Screlopterus coriaceus*

4

5

6

GLOSSARY

cerci—two sense organs that extend from the tip of an insect's abdomen. (pp. 11, 14)

exoskeleton—an insect's hardened outer skin to which muscles are attached and which protects its soft, internal body parts. (pp. 12, 16)

file—a rough edge with many tiny ridges on the underside of one of the cricket's front wings. (pp. 22, 23)

metamorphosis—a process of development during which physical changes take place. Complete metamorphosis involves four stages: egg, larva, pupa, and adult. Incomplete metamorphosis has three stages: egg, nymph, and adult. (p. 6)

ovipositor—an egg-laying tube which extends from the tip of an insect's abdomen. (pp. 14, 28)

palpi—small, movable feelers used for detecting nearby food sources. (p. 30)

scraper—a hardened vein on the upper side of a cricket's wing opposite the wing on which the file is located. (pp. 22, 23)

sounding board—a smooth area near the middle of the cricket's front wings, which amplifies sound. (pp. 22, 23)

spiracles—openings in an insect's abdomen used for breathing. (p. 16)

tympanums—ear membranes found on the front legs of grasshoppers and crickets. (pp. 22, 24)